Colors OF my Within

65 Poems from the Age of Innocence

EDMOND BRUNEAU

BOSTON
·B·
BOOKS

ISBN: 978-0-9616683-6-5
Library of Congress Control Number: 2011906357

Cover Design: Edmond Bruneau
Illustration: Lisa Zador

To my parents,
Pierre and Bernadine,
who always gave
me unconditional
love and support
even if they
didn't always
understand
their unusual son.

FORWARD

Between the ages of fifteen and twenty-one, I possessed the heart of a poet.
I wrote poems. About life. About war. About love. About growing up. In the
midst of raging hormones and a lust for living, poetry became my way of
sorting it all out. This was my age of innocence.

Reading them again after all these years was a great exercise. It was fun to look
back upon how I thought. How I felt. How I wrote. Some of the poems are quite
poignant. Some are serious, others are a little silly. But I do hope you will
consider these 65 poems together as a whole piece of work. They paint a clear
picture of who I was – and give a glimpse of the person I would become.

Perhaps these poems will find their way into other innocent hearts. Or perhaps
they will be an inspiration to others who have poetry in their soul but hadn't
written it down. Yet.

To keep things simple – and perhaps to fulfill my Virgo sense of harmony,
I placed these poems in alphabetical order. So, please don't appraise the
book by its first few poems. You might have at least one that speaks to you in
there – somewhere.

POEMS

A Cold Beach

Once upon a sunny day
when even waves
splash their salty heart away,
your body rests aground awhile
watching children
play castles,
sand on sand –
and all the people smile.

But today
is a beach
without a sun –
too brisk for swimming
too cold to run.
No castles. No smiles.
Nary a one.

For once the beach
is quiet
to ponder,
to think
a thought and tie it.

One can wonder
until
the rays of sun
are again cast upon
the freshened sand again
and begin
what life's begun.

A Letter from a Rejected Love

What is beauty?
Is it
a pale blue sky
embroidered against
the crimson sun?
Is it
distant
white mountains
blended with
green valleys and
golden hills?

Shades of trees
and leaves
leave a silhouette
of darkness that
shadow the blacktop street.
Yet,
a street passes before me
and I see nothing.

Frost and snow
embalms me
with its cold –
cleaning the earth
with its soft
white blanket.
Yet,
flowers still bloom.
And ice
cracks the road.

The beauty of
the sea
the hills
the valleys
remain.

Yet,
my heart
goes on
beating.

The winter
you gave me
was unwanted.
But it
seasoned me.
And now,
I see
more
clearly.

A Matter of Miles

How many mountains
of magical, mystical
misery
are among
the trail of knowledge?
Congratulate the boy
as he faces the world.
He just came out of college.

"I've been robbed!" he said.
"Where's my job?" he said.
Poor slob.
Go sob.
And face another mountain.

It was something to learn.
He couldn't start
at the top of the tower.
No prestige.
No power.
Nose against the grindstone.
Minimum wage an hour.

"I'm through," he said.
"No more climbing," he said.
"I have a home."
"A phone."
"Money for my bread."
"But I'm still a little lonely," he said.
Get a pack for your back and
face another mountain.
Matrimony.

"I'm through," he said.
"I have a home."
"A phone."
"A wife."
"A queen size bed."
"Now I can do something wild," he said.
Sorry.
Now you have a child.

How does it feel to
earn so much and
not have a single dime?
Every time you take a step
there are new mountains to climb.

Life is a matter of miles.
Of mountains. And plains.
It's all a matter of passages
and trekking the terrain.

A Message

Sing a song to me
ancient sea.
Your musical breeze
carries a creed
like a passage
in a symphony.

Conduct music for me,
stubborn sea.
Shore percussion
hisses with the
roll of the snare.
Sounds of eternity
everywhere.

My quiet breath
is too loud
for the chorus.
Clarion gulls
lend voice
to their ovation.

I hear my own mistakes
marking time to your
musical measures.
I listen to
your continual melodies
and wish it a treasure
I could save.

Why doesn't
my heart
beat to the
rhythm of the waves?

A Song of Solitude

Sometimes I wonder why
my life goes along
like pieces
without the pie.
Every problem seems to
multiply
and tumble
end over end
as if
the sun will never set
or trees will never get
a chance
to revel in the wind.

A win
is just a stroke of luck
a loss –
fragments of inertia.
No matter what
the win will cost,
the loss can
only hurt you.

A fool will pass it up,
not knowing his own
beginning or end.
What matters is if
his dinner's by six,
clothes are bought,
and every thought
of personal happiness
sought.

I try so hard –
reading rules
and keeping cool,
not to be the fool.
But sometimes
it's difficult to
play the stone –
when it erodes
and blows away
to play
with the sun and stars
and I am so alone.

Seems like the lights
will still
turn on
and off
and I will still
sputter
and cough
until I render the end.

I often wonder why
every leaf will
leave the tree,
like a man
without a friend.
I can only be
what I can only be.
And I will face
eternity
no matter what
lies around the bend.

A Thought Inside the Wind

Softly whisper
and gently touched
by melodious silence
and the windish rush.

My heart
goes on beating.
Beating.
While I
watch the spot,
life goes on.
Without me
or not.

Can tomorrow be
a beginning?
Or will I still
leap along the
gentle breeze
not knowing
how to fly?
Passing days
and days
again
bye and bye.

My reaching arm
gathers dust.
And never
will the day come
when my wrist again
exceeds its grasp
to realize
how far it runs.

The future
is endless –
riding the wave
of happiness.
Or all of it
will bind
upon the
wretched trail
of a narrow mind.

Alone

Alone.
Thoughts
of heavy stone.
I smile
at people
passing by
and
smiles return –
but smiles
are all that roam.

I wonder
someday
if one smile
will stop
and talk
the day away –
and chip alone
my heavy stone.

Is there
somewhere
a bay of life
where
I could
skip my stone
to ease
my burden
and strife?
Skip my stone
to a
deep
deep
home?

No one
wonders.
No one
knows.
Until a
chip of stone
is flown,
nothing deep
is ever
known.

Astrology Affair

Once upon a starry night,
when even the stars
are heavier than light –
your seat is sat,
your back is flat
and you lay –
gazing the dark heavens.
Happiness can only be sought
far as the Milky Way.

The stars don't twinkle
like the did
when and then.
They stick out like pins
times ten
times ten.

There are no constellations.
No rhythm, rhyme or rules.
Gone is the Queen of Lions
the Bear
the Gemini duo.
I only see
my memories
of hot
and cold
and cool.
The times I was the president.
And times I was the fool.

I'm a lot wiser now.
I'm beginning to
feel
I've never known how
to be real.

Pluto, oh Pluto
your distant isles are set –
peering through
a scope with care.
But please,
dear friend,
don't let me forget
you're out there.

Autumn

A leaf can leave its home
to journey
toward unknown,
yet its destiny, like others,
will lay with his brothers,
not knowing its
fleeing fall
wasn't so free
after all.
Joining the pile of leaves.

To be raked.
Stepped on.
Dried out.
Rained on.
Sunbaked sacrificially.
Is this where the
leaf wanted to be?
Does it ponder why
it took flight
and left its security?

A final flutter.
As if its friends
would know the end.
But perhaps it
was just the wind.

Color turned.
Lesson learned.

Ballad of the Borrower

Borrowing money
from every
mother's son.
The raising debt
flies like the sun.
It doesn't
just hurt me –
but everyone.

I'll sweat my brow
with raging toil.
My feet plant
like roots
in soil.
I'll stay until
I bust my rake,
with all the
money
I can make.

Someday
I'll pay those callers
not in words
but with those dollars.
Then I can
quit and
roam
and ramble.
Free with
the world.
Never again
to gamble.

Boomerang

Tears flourish
at my bedside.
Where egos nourish
and deep souls
hide.

I throw it away.
But it haunts me
day after day.
Against the will of
the wishing cup,
I still reach down
and pick it up.

But wishing
is for the worn.
Young and free.
Old and torn.
No wish comes
from a mortal mind
before it's born.

Hidden fears.
Present tears.
The boomerang
always flew.
Don't reject it.
Or protect it.
But retrieve it.
Yourself
away from you.

Brand New World

Maybe
everything
will split
like an atom.

What lies ahead
we shouldn't dread
for the best
is yet
to come.

Troubles.
Tears and rubble.
Locked in a sack.
They'll be forgotten
as we pass our way
through tomorrow's day.
Forget and
never look back.

So when it seems
beyond our dreams
that all won't come to an end.
Remember love
is just a mile away.
A brand new world –
a bit of time
around the bend.

Broken Chains

Twilight lingers
a dismal shadow of
a blanket –
upon the voyage
of a chariot –
racing full sail
to meet
the smile of the morning.

Fortress of darkness
blinds the
passageway –
prays
the twilight.
Linger
longer
without movement –
fragile as a fawn,
hidden from the
rays of sunlight.

A snap.
A mistake.
It reads
the location
and alerts
the approaching
sunlight of perception.

The chains
between the hours
split from
the tug-of-war
of sober control.
Hurry and cast
the final
spade of soil
upon the
twilight grave.
Nothing
can hold back
the sun.

Bullseye

Heart veins bleed.
Friends are
lost
and tossed
for the one thing
he needs –
a bullseye.

He shoots.
Never waiting
or wanting
stepping stones.
He talks
about one more loan
and how much
he wants
a bullseye.

No one knows
what he'd give.
No one knows
how he'd live.
The sensation.
The desperation
for
a bullseye.

Luck – a ghostly stitch.
When he finally made
the perfect pitch,
no longer was he
quite as rich.

It's been a long time comin'.
When it came,
it ceased the drummin'.
Hearts broken,
friends lost,
the only thing
he ever got –
a bullseye.

Christmas Morning

The floor
has never been
so cold before.
I never knew
footsteps
could creak
so loud
as I creep
past the door.

The light is
so dim,
I can hardly see
the tree.
I feel all
the packages
and discover
the big one is for me.

The world is
full
of sleepy heads.
My Mother says
"Go back to bed!"
I'll never
go to sleep –
the big one is for me.

Day of Downs

Sometimes we need
a sad day
to overcome our
moral decay.
Whispering
soothing
perseverance
enlists
the
appreciation
of happiness.

Sometimes we need
a sad song
to feel what's felt
when hearts
will melt
reminiscing
what was wrong.

We play,
we laugh
we drink
from the golden cup.
Without the
day of downs
there would never
be an up.

Daydream of the Bellboy

"Ding!"
That ring!
A persistent thing.
Hauling shirts
and shoes
people wore
door to door.

The bags are demanding,
each a heavy load.
But a bellboy dreams
many dreams –
like hitting the open road...

...where valleys grow
with fresh plowed rows.
And the dinging stops
on mountain tops.
Beyond a hotel's
profitable gain,
there's oriental gods,
monsoon rain
and sugar cane.

The warm winds
of the
South Pacific –
where the natives
are friendly
and the food's terrific.

A cruise to the Baltic Sea –
relaxed to fish,
relaxed to sleep –
awakened by a thrush
singing a piccolo song
from an evergreen bush...

"Ding!"
That ring!
A persistent thing.

Dusk

Tenderness
perched upon
rolling hills
and the
sunken sun
drills deep
into infinity.

Stars begin their birth
in a sky
not yet dark but
full of brightness
from
sunlight memories.

Behold a stage
of in-between –
without
light of light
or dark of dark.

So begins a beginning –
which ends
for another start
of tomorrow.

Life has a dusk.
Tenderness by
shades of gray.
Surety of step
plays the
role
of in-between.

Even in the
past's sunny
memories,
you're a
channel
of twilight.

Seconds after
the bird nests,
dusk overcomes
until the morning.

Eager Beaver

I look far
and
straight
at
the
line of life.
But
I can't wait
to
find a knife
and slice
my way
to fate.

Evening

Shadows
disappear –
leaving other means
of furnishing light.
Manmade.
Some pray
of the day.
While others
find sight
in the night.
Another
playtime.
Another
slumber.
Things
wonder
in
deeper
meaning –
in the
evening.

Everyman Revisited

Man thinks
with education
and uses
relaxation
to provoke
an easier way.
The damage it causes
outweighs –
not that
what's lost
really has a say.

Comfort and rest
begin to crest
and crumble
what's provided.
Discovery acclaims
popular aims.
Manifest Destiny
sees not
the graves.

DDT. LSD.
are very plain to see,
while poison begins
to tear
water and air!

Observe and
conserve.
Your laxness
of eagerness
promotes
just another way
to kill the day.

With every
grain of sand,
suicide gives a hand
to
everyman.

Faith

Dream softly,
my dancing Israel.
Of open arms,
whispering words,
that comfort
the sentence of intense –
that waiting silence.

The sun
no longer
bids pleasure
with its rays.
Journey to the land
of honey and sand
in months that
crawl from days.

Peace in
memory of Israel.
Potion in disguise.
We need no magic
to greet our eyes.
The days grow
longer with my sighs.

Dream again
my Israel.
When borders
won't exist.
When rest
will be
breath against
my chest.

My crusade
will be my caravan.
To return to the
land again
will be my exodus.

Focus of Love and Confusion

I stare at my watch
but I still
don't know the time.
I eat my
cheese and peanuts
and drink my tea –
yet my hunger
is unsatisfied.

Music encircles me.
Blurred are the
song vibrations
that beat
at my ear.

I feast upon nuts
cracking only
the empty shells.

The only impression
I make
is from my own
teething grindstone.

I shutter and
click like a camera –
picking up
only what light
has shadowed upon.

I dream
and fall asleep.
My weak batteries
project my
memories dimly –
And the
emptiness
in my heart
has no blood.

The bird has
flown away –
leaving a cold nest
or a
new life.

Forest of the Miners

Deep inside dark earth's burrows
man picks his precious silver
to find the key
that unlocks his world of
happiness, hope and glee.

Dark below a miner's feet
lies a crevice
he walks to meet.
He thinks of all the
money he craves
as he steps unsurely –
one foot in the grave.

A scream is heard –
the haunts of past.
Card games can
reap money fast.
A selfish life
is suddenly precious
when it
wants to last.

Deeper and deeper
metal and miners tell,
while getting
closer and closer
to a hotter and
hotter hell.

Glass

It's not easy
to sit and watch
pieces of glass beliefs
shatter before your eyes.
But what happens when
you stop taking
the sips of wine
inside your grasp
of that glossy glass?
What happens
when your mind
says hello
less times than
a thousand goodbyes?
What more could be tomorrow
than yesterday's dream disguised?
What happens when
you fight alone as
the fruit against the flies?
And when more pieces
shatter
no longer expecting surprise?

Expect the pain
as it begins to rain.
Shatter the glass
but let it pass,
like clouds blowing about the sky.
Don't cast your fate
to the wind
without first making it fly.
Pick up the pieces
you left behind
and glue the glass together
the way it fits your mind.
Nothing is long standing
if it cannot bend.
Don't be afraid of
letting it shatter
if you also let it mend.

Good Night

Kiss the stars good night.
Tell the
children of the swans
you'll see them
when it's light.

Part with fond embrace –
the mountains
the trees
the lakes.
Plead what it takes
to get away
and warm their
hearts of sorrow.
You'll return –
as everyday –
bringing a
bright tomorrow.

Hug and quiet
the sounds of night.
Crickets chirp
a lullaby.
Now is the time
all will part
until the ray of light.

Go to sleep
my friends of earth –
until you see the sun.
How hard the
last word seems,
when two
must part from one.

Kiss again,
stars good night
and hope this time
all will be right
when awakened
to the dawn.

I Am

I am a pacifist.
I am a shelter.
I am an island
with waves searching for a shore.
I breathe wind
yet it blows on through
and I am few.
I am many
as stars in the sky
or sand in the hand.
I am fruit to the hungry.
I am honey.
I am rain.
I am the collector.
I am the junkyard.
I am every side
yet see too much.
I am salvation.
I am damnation.
I am a speck of dirt.
I am the universe.
I am the roots of hope
the lakes of tears
the loss of love
the gain of blood.
I am the kettle of destiny
cooking goodness
for no one.
I am the grave
laid to rest in my pain.
I am the seed.
I am the target.
I am the pearl of persistence.
I am the tree of treachery
cutting against the grain.
I am the seep of sadness
leaking from a half-full barrel.
I am silicon.
I am suction without the grip.
I am above the sea.
I am rock.
I am.

I Too Have Seen the Sun

I too, my friend,
have seen the sun.
Where its rays
fell upon many a soul.
And many a heart
was won.

It's a sun that
will never set.
Nor will it
dare forget.
Plentiful.
Lasting.
Shining the
silent showcase.
Cueing the
director's casting.

The sun will rise
for every man
at different times
and different lands.

Inner peace!
Proclaims the rays
of harmony.
Every heart
will find its place
and show its face
and perish its
deeper moaning.

Onward to tomorrow,
on a cloudy, dismal day.
Each heart
will find its way
to live. To love.
And bask in
life's warm rays.

In a Heartbeat

I've lived
through
another day –
facing my perils
and chasing my
thoughts astray.

It always
comes close.
Thin is the
line between
life and death.
How quick
the moment.
The stifling
of breath.

Accidents
come and go
and we stick to
life like glue.
It can
occur in a
heartbeat.
But it just
can't happen
to you.

People pass
like spores
blowing in
the wind.
As you
grow wings
and soar,
you'll soon
discover
you too can
be a spore.
The carefree
thoughtless
breezy ride
may end
in
gruesome gore.

Journeys

Footsteps crack crisp forest fodder
and break them into segments smaller.
Journeys extend the common runner
whose footsteps crush fallen leaves
closer to another.

Shadows grow
as footsteps go
darker into each unknown.
Journeys narrow
the familiar hallows
spanning distance
apart from home.

It's always night.
It's always cold
and damp
from forest travel.
Yet, what difference
are the footsteps
that fall upon the
cold and dark arrival?

Slowly like syrup.
Gently like grace.
Soft light halos
new found meadows
growing at an unstepped pace –
as unusual
as journeys.

Memories, like sea water
roll silently into one another
and flow from tide to ebb –
shallow pools of
what was said.

Light
as bright as –
maybe brighter than
the place where home
and distance span.

Far from the forest now
clutching the today
And the tide, ever retreating —
Time and journeys
restlessly wait to return
to travels beginning.

Dark again
the forests now
as footsteps crack
crisp forest fodder.
Journey home
leaving fallen leaves
ground closer to another.

Shallow pools
of what was said.
Home memories, like sea water
find the tide
had left the shoreline unchanged
but nothing other.

July 4th

Firework prices
fly higher
than the contents,
as buyers inquire
"How potent?"

Less and less
we celebrate greatness
with flares and fire
safe and wise,
so no one ponders
why inflation can rise.

Up in smoke.
Our country
spends billions
on Earth Day,
but provides
only tradition
for its birthday.

Alas,
for this is the place we live!
How is it,
before the day's visit,
our Uncle Sam
has so much to give?

A nickel a flare,
penny a cracker,
now the
black market wares.
Smuggling for profit,
depending on the State.
All for us
to celebrate.

Kisses

My eyes say goodbye
to the
kisses of
the setting summer sun.
So many things
I haven't yet begun –
As moments
freeze into days
and time is
in suspension,
I don't have to
see if you are near.
I know.

Hypnotic stars
glisten
as they listen,
slowly soothing us
to sleep
together
at the same moment.

If I were a minstrel,
I wouldn't have awakened.
I would have lived forever
quietly
placidly
among the field of grass.
The dew.
Cold tears of a new day
falling upon my collar.
No more
are we hidden in
the shadows.

We haven't moved
since the evening
and it's sad
soon
I must be leaving.

A man is not a man
remaining shallow
in the gallows
and dwelling in
tenderness forever.
I must
satisfy
the devils of destitute.
And then
fall back
into my
security of
softness.

My lips quiver
in a motion
to say
I love you.
You squeeze my hand
and your pulse
says
"Don't say it again.
I'll wait 'till the when.
I understand."
We couldn't be closer together.

Live

I laugh
sometimes
and
hurry
and
worry
about things
that don't ever pay.
No matter how
the pieces
fit together
they seem
to just
get in my way.

Solemnly I
sit and sigh –
staring at
clouds in the sky
and I wonder –
just wonder –
if what I have
is here to stay.
Or if
it would be a
better thought
if I
lived for today.

My nerves
cling together
like
wrinkling leaves.
My mind
is wound up
by a dozen keys.
My every plan
is no more
than a
muffled sneeze.
I'm tired.

Damn tired.
Of being
too busy to see
the breeze
blowing through
the trees.
Then I smiled.
No one can
flee the future.
Facing you,
fortune –
although many dread,
is an unpleasant duty.
Like burying
the dead.

So I bear
the grief.
The stabs.
The sorrow.
And I say
"Live for today."
But I come from
the aches
of yesterday.
Remembering also
to
live for tomorrow.

Miss Pollen

Sensuous sachet.
Eminent scent
of delicate bouquet.
Perceptual perfume
of palatial wonder.
Nocturnal nuisance
blanketed by your silence.
Your infatuating incense.
My flower of the slumber.

The light of day
detects my fortune.
Subtle scent of
rancid roses.
Spicy stench to
castrate noses.
The dilemma of
bitter honey.
My snapdragon of the daylight.

Mood

What is the matter with me today?
Why can't I kiss your closeness?
Where is my smile?
And where is yours?

A tear.
A tear prevents
the ship to sail.
The notes to play.
The words to rhyme.
Sad.
But I don't have a reason to cry.

Don't despair over
this damn devil.
Keep your heart away
and cover me with
understanding.
My heart still cares.
But nothing can speak
while it's thinking.

Reassure
another day
will appear
and remember that
the lake of love
can't be drained
by a single tear.

Until I can gasp the
air again,
stay near.

My Lady of the Island

Run to the sky
dear lady.
Envision the sea
without
the storm
and the land
wild and free.

Grace each
coral form,
for in your mind
is where reefs
are born.

Smile upon
the sunshine.
Glowing rays
of warmth
upon a
sandy shore.
Life tries
its turmoils.
Smiles can
exist
during the
tough trials
in store.

Run to the sand
dear lady.
Your fate is
always near.
Every footprint
leads to
adventure –
if you proceed
without fear.

Remember
that you
control the clouds –
and you
will always dance.
Every bit
of magic
can be
tragic.
Great pain.
So please,
don't make it rain.

Run to the sea
dear lady.
All that has
passed
will
pass again.
The world
as we know it now
will never end.
Every secret
to love
and life
is just
around the bend.

My Sun

My sun rose gently today.
Its rays
forget their fashion;
provide energy for
my soft parade –
the roots of my compassion.

Smooth without
a whisper of a breeze,
my pond becomes a mirror.
The past is my reflection.
The future even nearer.
Ideals become my seeds.
I am new life.
My pollen is
a potion for my needs.
My flowers are my love.

Pick a flower and
keep it with care.
Its beauty will
scent the air
everywhere.
Delicate petals
are its sensitivity.
Sap, like blood in veins
may only live a brevity.
Dying quietly.
Softly.
Sadly.

Another venture for
the measure of my mind.
My womb gives birth
and seeks its own
love to find.
My sun sets with a smile.
Its rays won't forget
to add warmth
before
the final pardon.
The final fate.

Ocean

Noisy surf
and
silent sand
slide together.

Seaweed tickles
depth ridden shells,
while bolders
nurse the pebbles
on the
saturated shore.
And the bay birds
kiss
the pearled sky.

Crustacean beds
wait for humanity
to stir their slumber.
Tears are shed
by washed up elements
that once
were fully emerged.

Mysterious
as it is,
contentment
will be reached
at the horizon
where the sky
meets the sea.

On a Track

Ever since that day
I can't capture
reality
with a sweep of my hand.
Tears fall astray
inside my skin.
And my
thoughts
are within.

I'm different now.
And so are you.
What I find
is deep in my mind.
Storing the old
and the new.

My thoughts
are captured sunshine,
mellowed by an
Autumn leaf.
Together we had a
good time.
Alone,
I touch the grief.

My sorrow sulks
until the morn –
and without the sun,
my soul is
battered and torn.

I'm here.
But I'm lost.
So I move
place to place.
Searching for the
measure of life it costs.
And traveling
toward my grace.

Out on a Limb

What is it like
to see what's right
in a
completely
different
world?
It's as hard
to understand
as how
an oyster
creates a pearl.

Another world
of flowers
of thought
of depth
of mind
of touch.
What deed of hell
did I commit
to love
that world
so much?

My heart sings
that my world
was fine.
Living happy.
Peace of mind.
What binds
these ties
to this
love of mine?

A kiss.
Tender lips
of heaven
determine
a rendezvous.
What hand
of fate
can I
trust to thank
when wondering
the wonder of you?

It's lonely out here.
Out on a limb,
between the
worlds of us.
But I keep
hanging on
and pray
I can believe
everything.
I must.

It's a trait
of man
to pick and
choose
and wonder
if his
choice was right.
To win
and not to lose.
And not
give up the fight.

Passing Faces

In many places,
I see faces –
new
and old before.
A cage without
a key.
An open door.

Most
I never enter
but breeze along
tomorrow.
I listen to
the doldrums
but
never hold
its sorrows.

I
love
like
listen
learn
from
each new face
from every turn.
Some I grasp
and
their face
is in their place.
With these
I see
eternity.
None other
like no other –
with each its
speech and
personality.

They go
their own way
anyway –
not that I
would make a change.
But
somehow
somewhere
someone –
a stranger
won't be
so strange.

Concerns of the
coming day –
maybe of the week –
reflects an
expression
no one has
alike
on any street.

I'll never
reach the faces
who scatter
in
different places.
But in a crowd
of foreign faces,
the one or two
you meet
can be the mind's
single feat.

Peaks

Dew
kisses again
the leaves of life.
Sparkling against
the morning summer sun.
Peace
given time
mirrors the pool
of rational reflection –
the ripple of waves
against a personal shore.

Sunlight
peers though
the eyes of nature.
Knowledge never knew
how the sun was to shine.

Distant mountain –
a goal at the peak
seems far too clear
cut against
sky blue infinity.
All too few
worry about clouds
cluttering the view.
Many a heart
doesn't soothe
knowing mountains
don't move.

Lakes below
the distant climb
glisten and
shimmer with success.
Glacial giants
diminish
the rays of the sun.

The journey is
far too long
to worry about
the length of day.
Many a peak
is too far away
to tempt a step
to run.
No matter where
our feet may lead,
they have only
just begun.

Pitter-pat

Pitter-pat go my eyes
across the
once blue skies
and misused ocean.

Pitter-pat go my feet
running over
desolate souls
and
flattened mountains.

Pitter-pat goes my heart,
entering the temple
of the war-god,
with sanctuary of
bullets
rifles
and bombs.

Pitter-pat drips the water
from broken pipes
onto unused cars –
a sporadic rhythm
like drumbeats in
a gusty wind.
But without the natives.
And without the wind.

Pitter-pat falls a ball
off a concrete shelf
never to
bounce again.

Pitter-pat cracks an egg.
Fertile, but fried
a hundred times –
Not by a pan,
Pitter-Pat,
but by a bomb,
Pitter-Pat.
A bomb
they forgot to ban,
Pitter ----

Poems for the Prince
and Patches for the Pauper

My blood –
buttons on my shirt –
evidence
of my love
rich
in incidence.

I am but a prince
of eloping
my emotion.
Even if the
healing soap
never hardens
and I use
my only lotion,
nothing can stop
my love in locomotion.

I am but a pauper.
Wise but
bound in chains
linked to the
past of incidence.
Even with
experience since,
they can never
understand
all the knowledge
they let in
was chagrin.

Tomorrow unveils
truth of
yesterday's tales.
I have no jewels
to be a prince –
too much pride
to be a pauper.
I don't want
to weigh
my way.
And nothing
but nothing
can stop her.

Running Blind

My hopes
are less
victorious.
I climb hills
but can never
reach the
mountains.
Clustered are
my ideas –
dwindled in
my hell
of paradise.

Sick of Brick Walls

My body yields
so much
love to share
I shake
when I realize where I am.
But my visions
never appear.
I give small
until I receive.

I only have
a matter of time
before I
BURST.

The glow
of happiness
is to give,
but the
signal of love
is to receive.

Still Waters

Still waters silence sleeps
stumble along
a mountain steep.
Sunlight in the morning.

Awake!
Etching light.
Burns sense from sight.
Burns retinas of reason.
Hears bright voices
but cannot see them.

Still waters flow
through their hands –
Portrays a painting.
Seeps the sand.
But still sighs
and dreams on
to another day
when shadows come.
Burying away
the burning sun.
A capsule of
another season.

Coolness cries
its reveille.
Sunlight becomes
a brevity.
Still waters escape
fiery ration.
Leaving a pool
among its passion.
Shadows grow from
their compassion.

A lofty farewell to
the sheriff of sunlight.
The death of sunlight.
The birth of love brings
mocking to the mourning.
Stars smile
as it rests awhile.
Beyond the rift
of remembrance
dies the shadows
of the morning.

Sunset

If and when
silent sun
sets between
two sleeping moons –
never letting
peace slip by
to play against
the piper's tune.

Music of meadows creep –
plains, forests,
mountains, lakes.
The snarled sea,
harp of the deep,
play the rays
to quake
the break.

The gleam lasts
with a supporting cast –
molten fire on sandy snow.
High up
on mountain top,
the fireball gives
its second show.

Clouds pinken
as the skies comply
with embarrassment
as light goes by.
Since the dying sun
has passed,
a funeral
dark and black
amass.

From the darkness
sparkling stars
become.
But only after
the setting sun.

Susceptibility

In the grassy fields
of pathless plains
lay the roots of
the future –
nourished by
seasonal rains.

Rigid souls
who flex
their sails
splinter from
nature's
turbid gales.

Like waves
rolling the
desert floor,
people bend
from shore to shore.
Others who fight
and stand their ground
break by the breeze
that blows around.

The flexible society
will always stay
to bend its
meek
and lowly way.

Unless a fire
destroys the grass,
nothing happens
or even harass.
If the flame
continues to burn
and ruins the things
mankind has earned,
then it too
will surely pass
without
the fuel
to
let it last.

Testament of a Pioneer

I've loved to see the morning sun
and listen beyond
what the birds would sing.
Pass through the grass
as I swiftly run,
while winding along
like a ball of string.

I wish my heart again
could stand a walk,
more less a run.
But age plays a deadly game
that wears my eyes
and makes me lame.
Leaving only
the ghost
of the morning sun.

Someday, I say
I'll pass away –
but it won't be age
that steals my numbered days,
but the sound of
death's gun –
the longing lapse
of the morning sun.

The Gap

I'm still across the river from you.
Close, but so far away.
A separation beyond my grasp,
unless there is a way...

A bridge to my desires unknown.
Boat without its oars.
A river quiet – dark and deep,
never a turbulence soar.

We walk parallel the river together.
Laugh together. Sing together.
Seemingly endless, this river of time
'till it flows
into Lake Unprediction
where we separate away.

Yet, lakes are round
so if we are bound
by our memories –
and strive toward
each other to greet –
our souls
will softly meet.

The Meadow

Again
I approach the meadow.
Never did I think
I would ever see it again,
if but only through a window.

Yet I've returned
with a crutch full
of memories
and wisdom.
Gone is the innocence.
Gone are the insects
that bite and sting.
Found again is the meadow.
And I,
a broken wing.

And if
I am here to stay,
it will be
the cause
of understanding.
Clouds may rain
and the sky may shine
and again
the birds will sing –
if only someone
would mend my wing.

From here
I will sip
from the sovereign spring
and listen for the bells
that begin to ring.
Never had I thought
would I venture twain
and kiss again
something
closer
than
darkness.

The Much Needed Victory

Crusade to the
moment
of the evening.
Charge your
embattered bones
into the
battle
once more.
For only you
can win the war.

Straighten your tie.
Button your shirt.
All that you've
been through
can't much hurt
all that you've
been through
before.

It may
happen again.
No one can
shield
a broken heart.
And no one
can yield
the very part
that was
only beginning
to mend.

So open the door –
to wallflowers
and gypsies.
Soothe the
heart
that grows so sore
awaiting
the much needed victory.

The Risk of Being

Seconds tick away
everyday.
Time.
You can't grasp it.
It melts.
How many times
could you really
say something
and say
empty words instead?
Next time
you will say
what you feel,
right?
Too much bother.
Too much trouble.
Too little time.

What *is*
important
anyway?
What leaves
and
what stays?
What's given
and
what takes?
Ignore concerns
they're only
mistakes.

What do
you
really
care about?
What do you want?
What do you need?
What do you give?
A part of you –
or a raincheck?
Wet weather
we're having
isn't it?

The hardest
thing is to
grab the
sliver of soul
and share it.
It hurts.
It helps.
It's dangerous.
And
time consuming.
But it's your time.
And your danger.
And your world.

Feel the warmth
of another
brave soul.
Get nervous.
Explore
new territory.
That's the risk
of
being alive.

The Train

There is a train
that never stops,
to it
the journey
unknown.
When a station
comes into sight,
they refuse
to bury
his bones.

Onward
he roams.
Blood as fuel.
Tears as tracks.
And a heart
to guide it
alone.

In the distance,
he sees another stop
and prays
things might be
different here –
to help him home
from nowhere.

Clouds darken
with heavy rain.
There was
no one there
to hear the train.

There is a train
that keeps on
churning,
searching for
a stop to
the nowhere journey.
With only his
heart
to guide it
alone.

Time will Tell

Rapid falls the rain.
Farther and farther
dark clouds appear
from the
edge of end's terrain.

Someday
my thoughts
will be said –
and the
darkness,
cloudy and gray
will have
light
cast upon
instead.

When will the
brightness
appear once more?
To soothe my
fading
aching
heart
and patch
the tissue
it tore –

Time will tell
golden tales.
On top the
highest
mountain peaks.
And along
the endless trail.

Tomorrow

Let all men with shadows weep.
Let them mourn until the morn.
Remain still while chances creep.
A day rings anew –
And from the scorn
comes a different you.

Hours past, a
new tomorrow.
New hopes.
New dreams.
New pain.
New sorrow.

Things cannot
remain the same.
A different time
runs with the rain.
A different scene
has certainly sprung.
Each day
another game.
Plagued by the
telling tongues.

Express today
with thought –
because things
are bought
that shouldn't
have been sought
until tomorrow.
Don't wait.
Don't hesitate.
Tomorrow's fears
are
yesterday's tears.

Midnight is only a
part
of the start.

Try Again

What is there to lose
my friend?
What couldn't
you start again
that still might
possibly end?

So many times,
so many signs,
point to a
door that's open.
A speaker is just
another man
when his words
remain unspoken.

And a heart is just
another heart,
without knowledge
without pain –
it only then
remains unbroken.

So it's time to
try again –
Another trial.
Another trail.
Another tenderness.
And light the flame –
the warm candle
of interest.

Tuesday Evening, 10:16 pm.

Rest becomes
my exodus.
Warmth and
comfort relax.
My mind becomes
innocent –
while my thoughts
lay beside me
among
the bedroom walls.

Peace
is its own treasure,
suspended
within my dreams.
Lily softness
sweeps my feet.
My only thought
of dismay
is the
wretched awakening
to the sunlight
of tomorrow.

The sun
will rise again
as everyday.
Then I'll be
kidnapped
into the
hell world
of treachery –
Hiding in
the
underground cave
found only
in my dreams.

Gone
is the
sound of solitude.
The melancholy flute.
The bowl of grapes.
Gone is
the free figure
cast into
a corner of life.

Found
is the
tunnel of magic,
softly sprinkled
in my
sleepy sanctuary
of dreams.

Under a Willow Tree

My life
is under
a willow tree.
It sits
protected –
safe
isolated
neglected.

Branches droop
toward the ground –
leaf upon leaf
it
shades the grief.
While I lie
under the
darkened blight,
it shades
the light.

Outside
it's much too bright
to see
what's real
to see.

Outside
my neighbors
don't look
like
my serene stream
or babbling brook.

I'll never
set out
to set out.
I'll play
where I stay.
Not bright and real,
but
cool and ideal,
while the
grass grows over me –
my shaded willow tree.

Uneasiness

Distant hills
chill with loneliness.
Deserts the trail
toward togetherness.

Is the hike too long
to follow some more?
Your back too tired?
Feet too sore?

Without the ease
of want to do,
very few
can follow through.

You're able to
approach the hills
with many a gap
and hike them
without a map –
A treasure
of pleasure
loosens the ropes
of uneasiness.

So when you discover
what trouble
you might find,
and listening
is the last thing
on their minds,
then hop
and walk
the trail away.
Day after day,
endless hills
you have
to climb.

Waiting for the Sun

I've lost
what others
have lost before.
I've won
victory
without
the war.
Maybe it's a dream –
the scene
of roses
climbing forbidden walls.
And a flute
playing a melody
of love –
while people
hear the call.
Maybe I've won
the final battle –
or maybe it's just begun.
I watch
because I'm waiting.
Waiting for the sun.

Shadows.
Only shadows of success.
It means
the in-between of
happiness and
bitterness.
For a shadow
is only a reflection
of men
pinching each other
off
for perfection.

We can't go back.
There is no
place in the past
where we
could live
without the
smell of powder.

No where to go
but up.
We sit
and wonder
what
can be done.
Many stand their ground.
Many fool around.
Many run.
I watch
because I'm waiting.
Waiting for the sun.

Wounds

If I've been
cut once,
I've bled
a thousand times.

Each time,
the band-aid
just covers up
the scabs and scars
that will stay
for a long
long time.

Do knives and bullets
hurt as much
as rejection
and treason?

My sorrows
cut deep
into the passion
of my heart.

You

You are the pearls
the twilight
evergreen meadows
and
salty air.

I am the ship
bound for
spices of the Orient –
the ruby
the emerald
the ring of Saturn
the ring of
little brass bells.
Worker bee
hopping
flower to flower
to build
its honey.

You are
light and night –
my shadow
my snow
my sunshine
my autumn leaves
my spring
my birth
my beginning.

With me
we are the
universe.
Without you,
an island.

You Can't Go Out the In Door

With busloads of
knowledge to send,
no one can recommend
mutilate or bend
a pathway to the
communication store –
since no doorman
is at the door.

Jailed ideas
without a key.
Graspless,
without a knob,
to unlock ideas
for eternity.
Indeed it is a
tiresome job.

Some men are meek.
Others are poor.
His problems are great
and he can't be late,
so his own solutions soar.
All at the risk of
the great debate
because
you can't go out the in door.

We speedily move along
with a one way door
that can lead us onto
the path of wrong.

Pondering people
plead a way out.
Results lead many to doubt
any certainty
for humanity.
Answers solve
questions galore
and many will be sound
if you
don't go out the in door.

EDMOND BRUNEAU